PORTFOLIO OF
TRADING SYSTEMS

PORTFOLIO OF TRADING SYSTEMS

Path of Least Resistance to Consistent Profitability

Teguh Pranoto Chen

PARTRIDGE

A Penguin Random House Company

To order additional copies of this book, contact
Toll Free 800 101 2657 (Singapore)
Toll Free 1 800 81 7340 (Malaysia)
orders.singapore@partridgepublishing.com

www.partridgepublishing.com/singapore

DISCLAIMER

Futures, forex, and options trading have large potential rewards but also large potential risks. You must be aware of the risks and be willing to accept them in order to invest in these markets. You should not trade with money you cannot afford to lose. This book is neither a solicitation nor an offer to buy/sell futures or options. No representation is being made that any account will or is likely to achieve profits or losses similar to those discussed in this book. The past performance of any trading system or methodology is not necessarily indicative of future results. This book is for informational purposes only.

Contents

PRAISE FOR THIS BOOK

If you want to learn more about trading systems, Teguh's book is a very good investment. He covers the full spectrum of systematic trading, from system design to money management. The trading business can be very difficult, but Teguh's book will reduce the learning curve considerably. Plus, Teguh is a trader himself and believes in the systematic approach. The book also touches on sophisticated topics, such as Monte Carlo simulation and optimization. In the end, the book shows the true benefit of combining noncorrelated algorithms to increase profits and reduce drawdown.
~ George Pruitt, Author of *The Ultimate Trading Guide* and *Building Winning Trading Systems with TradeStation*

An enjoyable read. Teguh gives well-considered insight into the foundations required to embark upon a successful trading career.
~ Trent Donovan, Broker

Teguh has crystallized his many years of trading experience into a few simple rules in this must-read book. I highly recommend it to those who want to succeed in a trading career.
~ Wang Tao, President, Technical Analysts Society (Singapore)

Mechanical trading is a complex topic and there are few book in existing literature that explain it simply and accurately for the newbie. Teguh has risen nicely to the challenge. In this straightforward and refreshing primer, he explains the ins and outs of computerized trading, how it works on paper and how it works in the demanding real world. From classic strategies to customized systems development, Teguh gives advice and insights born of his own hard-earned, successful track record in computer-based trading. A must-read for anyone wanting a fast and easy handle on mechanical trading.

~ Wai-Lin Terry, Fmr SVP,
Dresdner Kleinwort Benson Capital Markets (USA)

To my beloved wife, Kim,
and my beautiful children, Lara and Zeke,
I dedicate this book of trading wisdom.

ABOUT THE AUTHOR

Upon graduation, Teguh Pranoto Chen traded the opportunity of a lifetime to join one of the most respected investment banks in the world with assignments in New York, London, and Tokyo to surf in Hawaii. Returning to Asia, he started his career with P&G in Jakarta. Not long afterward, he skipped an offer to join a top-twenty Ph.D. program in the US. His assignments with P&G included shutting down manufacturing sites, delisting a publicly listed company, integrating new businesses, and streamlining operations, while building successful businesses across Asia. Along the way, he bagged multiple awards and recognitions.

Afterward, Teguh joined a privately funded start-up to build an integrated coal-mining project with three hundred kilometers of railway behind access to the second-largest coal mine in Indonesia. Currently with Publicis, one of the largest advertising holding companies, he embarks on a new challenge to build integrated digital business across Asia.

Teguh lives in Singapore with his beloved wife, two beautiful children, and their little dog. While not attending his day jobs, he dedicates his time to his passion for trading.

For more information, email tc@fultonholding.com.

The game of speculation is the most uniformly fascinating game in the world. But it is not a game for the stupid, the mentally lazy, the person of inferior emotional balance, or the get-rich-quick adventurer. They will die poor.
~ Jesse Livermore

CHAPTER 1

Great Traders Are Not Born; They Are Made

Legends, myths, and icons abound in the trading world. Traders especially revere the phenomenon of the Turtle Traders, an experiment initiated by Richard Dennis, a successful trader who became a millionaire before turning twenty-six. Dennis said that great traders were not born; they were made. All they had to do was follow a few simple trading rules, which could be easily taught and followed. As part of this experiment, Dennis took under his wing fourteen novices who had no trading experience. After training for two weeks, they went on to achieve rock star status by making $100 million in about four years in 1980s.

The story goes that the apprentices were called Turtles because Dennis told a *Wall Street Journal* reporter, "We are going to grow traders just like they grow turtles in Singapore."

Therein lies the heart of mechanical trading, that by adhering to a few rules to enforce discipline and quantify risk, great fortunes can be made. The Turtles employed a simple trend-following system, using indicators called a Donchian Channel, which will be illustrated later in this book, and traded across markets, such as commodities, currencies, and bond markets.

Mechanical trading has been around for decades. Its popularity has waxed and waned as markets do, but interest has returned in the past few years because of the availability of affordable computing power and highly sophisticated trading and analytical software.

Each trading system can be customized to adapt to different types of market conditions—a trending market with low volatility, a nontrending market with volatility, etc.—across a variety of time frames. Profitable long or short trades are possible not only in bull markets but also in bear markets. A trading system is designed to deliver a specific risk-return objective. A trader might tolerate higher risk, drawdown, and volatility for a higher expected return. Another trader might prefer low drawdown with a relatively lower expected return.

Trading systems hosted in the cloud are capable of running without any intervention 24/7 across geographies and assets classes. This is not something that can be easily achieved by discretionary traders. Signals can be generated for short holding periods, such as hours, or longer holding periods, such as days, weeks, or months.

Adding noncorrelated trading systems into a portfolio of trading systems improves risk-reward proposition. More importantly, the portfolio can produce more consistent results.

How many millionaires do you know who have become wealthy by investing in savings accounts?
- Robert G. Allen

CHAPTER 2

Speculation—A Risky Business?

Investing or Trading

The term *investing* is generally equated to a buy-and-hold approach of buying securities and holding them for long periods, such as months or years. Generally regarded as the greatest investor of all time, Warren Buffett is famous for holding his assets for indefinite periods. This is also perceived as a lower-risk strategy to grow wealth. Prior to allocating capital to a certain stock, a typical investor studies its fundamentals, such as the growth plan, projected EPS, and financial ratios.

Characteristics	Investing	Trading
Approach	Buy and Hold	Day Trade
Holding	Long Term	Short Term
Analysis	Fundamental	Technical
Risk Factor	Low Risk	High Risk

In contrast, the term *trading* is associated with shorter holding periods. Because of technological advancements, it is relatively easy to day-trade in the Internet era. Trading is perceived as a relatively high-risk strategy, especially with many people getting burned trying to get rich quick. A trader bases trade signals on technical analysis, e.g., price action, chart pattern, or mechanical trading.

Speculation

Merriam-Webster defines *speculation* as activity in which someone buys and sells things (such as stocks or pieces of property) in the hope of making a large profit but with the risk of a large loss.

A person involved in the stock market, either as a buy-and-hold investor or as a day trader, undoubtedly expects to profit from the activities. Additionally, both run a risk of a large loss. Following the definition from Merriam-Webster, it is probable that both investing and trading can be classified as speculation.

Some people reason that stock investing is a relatively low-risk activity. Perhaps it is not really speculation? Yet many buy-and-hold investors lost a significant portion of their investments during Black Friday, the dot-com bubble, the Asian financial crisis, and/or the recent sub-prime mortgage crisis.

In contrast, some people claim that trading *is* a speculation business. It is a well-known statistic that most (if not almost all) day-traders lose their initial capital in their first few months in the market. What is not well known is that a trader regards risk management as the most important objective in this endeavor.

Even the greatest investor who has ever lived, Warren Buffett, once famously said that there are only two rules for making money.

Rule No. 1: Never lose money.
Rule No. 2: Never forget Rule No. 1.

There is an old saying on Wall Street: "There are old traders, and there are bold traders, but there are *no* old, bold traders." While most people would name making tons of money as the main (and perhaps only) objective for dabbling in the stock market, the old and bold trader would disagree.

In his book *Trading for a Living*, Dr. Alexander Elder, a renowned world-class trader, defined how these old-and-bold traders systematically and religiously prioritize the speculation objectives:

1. **Minimize risk; preserve capital.**
2. **Make small but consistent profit.**
3. **Once in a while, make a killing.**

In conclusion, any person involved in the stock market *is* a speculator. The most important lesson is neither debating about the terms investing versus trading nor defining the term speculator but rather comprehending that risk management is the key to success. The man generally regarded as the most famous speculator who ever lived, Jesse Livermore, blew his account twice for not managing risk. While Warren Buffett (an investor) and Dr. Alexander Elder (a trader) differ on their approach to the market, they are in alignment in their position on risk.

Logic will get you from A to B.
Imagination will take you everywhere.
~ Albert Einstein

CHAPTER 3

About Technical Analysis

Growing Wealth

A commonly understood approach to growing wealth is to allocate available funds in a certain proportion of stocks, bonds, and cash or cash equivalents. Based on fundamental analysis, financial advisers recommend various sectors, geographies, and asset classes to fit clients' individual investment objectives. As time passes, these allocations are adjusted to rebalance the portfolio to match the investor's stage of life. More is allocated toward bonds and cash or cash equivalents, and less is allocated toward stocks.

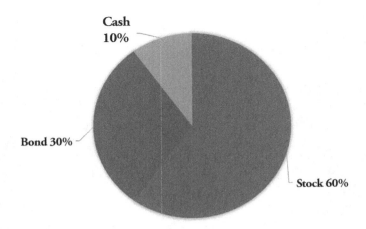

Illustration of conventional asset allocation

In recent years, property investment has become more popular and is growing in importance in portfolio management. This is especially true in growing and developing countries where property prices are widely believed to increase consistently. In search of higher returns, available capital may even be allocated to gold funds, agriculture funds in faraway places, and even swallow farms. The quest to find nontraditional investment vehicles is a never-ending story.

Technical Analysis

In contrast to fundamental analysis, neither financial ratios nor growth plans matter in technical analysis. Price is the single most important decision-making variable for technical analysis.

A *discretionary trader* looks at a chart and interprets it, whether it symbolizes a cup and a handle, a triangle, or even a house and two peaks. If the chart pattern is known, then a decision can be made to buy or sell. For most, discretionary trading can be described as the art of speculation, as trading decisions are made from the gut. What some see as a cup-and-handle formation may look like a random chart to others.

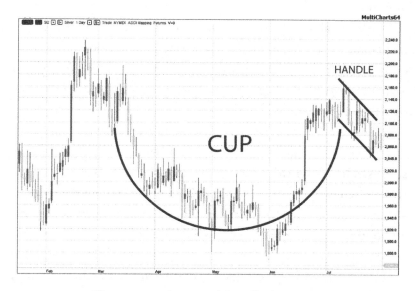

Illustration of cup-and-handle formation

A *mechanical trader* manipulates historical price data to find potential patterns that can be developed into a trading system. The development relies on objective reasoning (*logic and rules*) and statistical analysis (*data mining*). The results are verified to build confidence that the system will perform reasonably well. As such, mechanical trading can be described as the science of speculation, because trading decisions are based on a statistically proven hypothesis.

Logic and Rules

In his book *The Psychology of Trading* (2006), Dr. Brett Steenbarger, a psychologist and trader, notes that winning traders are "rule-governed." Those who come out ahead use trading rules to guide their trading and to help them maintain a positive frame of mind.

Rules establish the conditions for entry and exit that must be met before a trade is carried out. When these conditions are met, the odds tilt in favor of the trade. Over time, these odds translate into a growing *equity curve* (a graphical depiction of a trading account over time).

How about the psychological benefit? Rules reduce ambiguity and produce less stress. Trade occurs when the system produces signals. Think of it this way: It is much easier and safer to cross the street when the pedestrian signal is lit up because cars have come to a stop. A trader who flies by the seat of his pants is like a pedestrian attempting to cross the highway—it is totally nerve-wracking!

The rules are meant to provide competitive advantage, but they have to be based on the trader's personal understanding. This is where creativity comes in. An idea can be based on an observation that gaps at the open on high volume lead to higher prices during the day. Or it may be based on the belief that strong market trends start with a ten-day high. Profitable ideas can come from anywhere, such as trading forums, blogs, magazines, seminars, or Bloomberg.

Tip: Successful traders are intellectually curious and never stop learning. Investment in learning new skills is part of the cost of doing business.

It is important to match trading rules to the trader's personality. Some traders may be more risk averse than others and hence prefer to make small but consistent profits. Others may prefer a holding time of fewer than thirty minutes in intraday trading because they want to be in cash every night and not risk unexpected market volatility.

There are three kinds of lies: lies, damned lies, and statistics.

~ Anonymous

CHAPTER 4

What is a Trading System?

Investopedia defines a trading system as a group of specific rules, or parameters, that determines entry and exit points for a given equity.

Characteristics of a Trading System

- Defines precise sets of trading rules (entry and exit).
- Provides trading signals when prescribed conditions are fulfilled, such as when and at what price to enter or exit a trade.
- Designed to be executed without taking human emotion into consideration.

Why a Trading System?

A well-designed trading system provides a statistically meaningful way to minimize risk before risking capital in the market. Based on the analysis, a trader knows its risk-reward expectation, probability of winning, and even estimated average length of a trade. This is particularly comforting information for those who prefer data-based decision making.

A set of rules eliminates the need for discretionary trade decisions. It has been proven time and again that human fear and greed are damaging to the bottom line.

Every system is designed to match the trader's risk appetite and personality. Some may prefer a system with a high winning ratio despite its relatively moderate annual return. Others may prefer a system with a low winning ratio that yields a potentially higher annual return. In the end, it is all about personal preference.

In a more advanced stage, a combination of trading systems, commonly called a portfolio of trading systems, can actually improve the risk-reward ratio. Returns grow, but risk should grow at a slower rate. It is an excellent way to diversify and to smooth out equity-curve progressions.

Past performance of a system is *not* an indication of future performance. Even a well-designed system will fail someday, somehow. An old adage from Wall Street captures this perfectly:

The largest drawdown of a strategy
is always in the future.

Tip: Always be prepared for double the drawdown estimated by the trading system.

Benefits of Mechanical Trading

1. It removes emotion from the trading decision-making process, and it promotes consistency among decisions.

Emotions are the greatest enemy of successful trading because they cause destructive behaviors, such as second-guessing, impulsive trading, and reckless decision-making. Removing emotions from entry and exit decisions and basing them on a disciplined, systematic approach is the major benefit of mechanical trading.

In discretionary trading, a trader in a position that hits a record high has to weigh whether to hold on for further upside or liquidate to lock in profit. Similarly, the trader in a losing position has to consider whether to hold on for potential recovery or liquidate to minimize loss.

2. It quantifies risk and reward and matches trader appetite to acceptable risk.

   The risk-reward ratio is known prior to entering a trade. One trader may be comfortable with a 1:3 risk-reward ratio, while another trader may prefer a 1:5 ratio. Similarly, one trader can handle a system with a 30:70 win-loss ratio, while another may only execute a system with better than an 80:20 ratio.

3. It provides a means to test the reliability of a trading idea in a statistically meaningful way without having to risk capital in the market.

   Tips and theories are more than abundant in the market. However, few actually work out well. The method used by Richard Dennis and the Turtles was profitable several decades ago. However, the same concept tested by a trading system shows that it no longer works in today's environment.

4. It promotes diversification to improve return without significantly increasing risk.

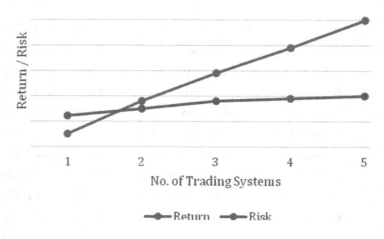

Drawbacks of Mechanical Trading

1. Every trading system fails someday, somehow. It is a question of when, not whether, the system will fail. As such, past performance is no guarantee of future results.

2. It takes time and effort to learn the ropes. It takes five years of medical school plus two years of on-the-job training to groom a doctor. It takes years to shape an aspiring trader into a trader. It takes even longer to transform a trader into a successful trader.

3. Every rule has to be translated into code that your computer can understand. Your computer then runs your trading rules through your trading software, which looks for trades that comply with your rules. Wrongly coding a rule, not being able to detect a logic error, or not sufficiently testing a system can lead to massive losses.

Tip: Developing a profitable system may take months, if not years. Nevertheless, a well-designed system can yield profitable results for years to come.

Success is not final; failure is not fatal.
It is the courage to continue that counts.
~ Winston Churchill

CHAPTER 5

Key Success Factors

Self-proclaimed gurus preach about how to make money in the stock market. Yet, nothing is true except the conventional wisdom of methodology, money management, and mental fitness. Dr. Alexander Elder (1993) called these the 3Ms.

Methodology — It may be based on tarot cards, the position of the moon in the solar system, or even, in this case, technical analysis. Whatever it is, a trader has to have an approach to trade. Success comes from trading a well-tested system. Often, the best systems are those with the simplest rules.

Money Management — In the simplest terms, this is about knowing when to cut your losses and when to let profit run further. More important is the concept of position sizing, optimizing risk and reward through strategic management of the size of each position.

Every trade and its risk decision is considered in relation to the overall portfolio.

Mental Fitness — Probably the most abstract concept, mental toughness is considered by many to be the most important component of the 3Ms. It means sticking with the system and keeping the faith even in the deepest drawdown, knowing that it is still within the system parameters and will be back. It means pulling the trigger according to signals generated by the system without having a second thought.

Regardless of the debate over which component of the 3Ms is most important, it is important to realize that none works in isolation. All three must be in harmony for a trader to see growth in his or her equity curve.

The Holy Grail

Every trader is looking for the Holy Grail, the perfect system that works every time to bring in untold wealth. While no system is perfect, these are engines that make mechanical trading a superior approach to building wealth.

Profit = Precision x Frequency x Leverage

Precision — In longer periods and over a significant number of trades, a well-designed system should deliver with precision, within its parameters, and with few variations. It is much easier to put extra capital to work when you know that the system is stable and will likely be consistent in meeting your expectations.

System	Yr 1	Yr 2	Yr 3	Yr 4	Yr 5	Avg
A	15	20	11	18	26	18
B	-10	50	-25	75	35	25

System B has delivered a better average of 25 percent in the past five years, but the result is rather erratic. In contrast, System A has delivered a lower average of 18 percent but without a significant fluctuation from year to year. In terms of compounding, taking frequency and leverage (below) into consideration, System A is a much more powerful system.

Frequency — To grow initial capital of $100,000 to $500,000 within three years requires an annual return of at least 71 percent. Assuming a 70:30 win-loss ratio and an average of ten trades per year, each trade has to yield more than 10 percent to deliver the expected annual return of at least 71 percent. However, with a 70:30 win-loss ratio and an average of one hundred trades per year, each trade has to yield only more than 1 percent to generate the same annual return.

Leverage — This is a double-edged sword. Used properly, it compounds positive returns. It is not unusual for a seasoned trader to secure 1:100 leverage for trading index futures or 1:1,000 for trading currencies. A consistent yield of at least 0.1 percent per trade is much more meaningful to the bottom line with leverage. In contrast, used in the wrong way, leverage can easily ruin the account.

You were born to win, but to be a winner,
you must plan to win, prepare to win, and expect to win.
~ Zig Ziglar

CHAPTER 6

The Game Plan

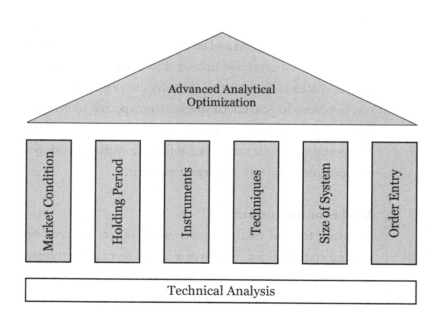

Trade What You Can, Not What You Want

Know thyself! A trading system should reflect the trader's personality, preference, and style. A trader who enjoys watching the market tick by tick may consider a day-trading system. In contrast, a trader who lacks concentration in monitoring the market may not do well with the same system. Hence, the trading system is built to match the person, not the other way around.

Key Considerations in Building a System

Each choice has its own consequences. There is no perfect choice, but choices must be made.

1. **Objective**
    Start with a goal in mind and be mindful of the consequences. The goal can be expressed in several terms, such as expected return, risk level, smoothness of equity-curve growth, or any combination. In general, the higher the expected return, the higher the risk that has to be tolerated. A goal to earn at least 100 percent per year return is not feasible with a drawdown expectation of at least 10 percent per year.

2. **Market or instrument**
    Some are fond of trading stocks, while others are keen on trading commodities. Similarly, each market or instrument has its own peculiarities, its behavior, and its pluses and minuses. Choose wisely and stay with the choice. Nothing is more harmful to the account than trading things you don't understand. It is important to start with one market or instrument and master it well before venturing to other areas.

3. **Holding period**

   Jesse Livermore, considered the greatest trader who has ever lived, once said that *the big money is made by the sitting and the waiting, not the thinking.* The longer the holding period of a trade, the greater the profit potential, the lower the number of potential trades, and the bigger the expected drawdown. A trigger-happy trader may be attracted to the action in day trading, but he or she has to realize that the money is made in a longer time frame.

4. **Initial capital**

   Trade with caution; trade only with funds dedicated for trading. A trader who trades with scared money, money that is required to support his or her daily expenses or family, is greatly impacted in his or her decision making. Greed to win and fear of losing cloud the trader's judgment.

It is not the beauty of a building you should look at;
it's the construction of the foundation
that will stand the test of time.
~ David Allan Coe

CHAPTER 7

Pillars of a Trading System

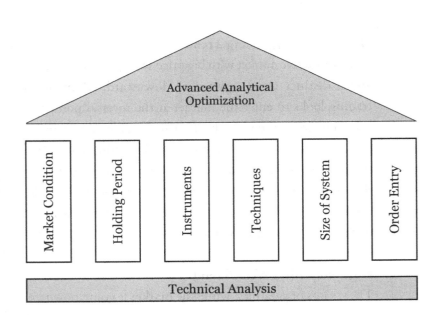

Market Condition

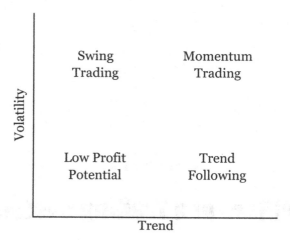

Illustration of volatility and trend determining market condition

1. **High Volatility, Strong Trend**

   This is an active market with big price swings, strong volume, and a distinct trend upward or downward. Momentum trading looks to enter the market at the reversal point and ride the trend accordingly. In this market, an adaptive technique and a combination of trend-following and swing-trading works well. Adaptive technique uses trailing stops that adjust according to the price movement. Riding the trend in a relatively short time frame means capturing profit in the volatile trending market.

2. **High Volatility, Weak Trend**

   There's lots of volatility, while the market is going nowhere. It is a much more challenging environment that is best served with oscillators and other short period indicators.

3. **Low Volatility, Strong Trend**

   The market is trending accordingly with relatively low volatility. This is where trend-following techniques prevail, such as moving average crossover and channel or band indicators. The trader uses moving average crossover to signal the beginning of a new trend or the end of a trend. Similarly, action is taken when price breaks a channel of a band.

4. **Low Volatility, Weak Trend**

   This is a dull, sideways market with few opportunities. Under such conditions, a variety of option strategies is the most promising technique.

Market conditions are rapidly changing. Trend following, which worked so well in the past three decades, has lost its magic in the past several years. The chart on the next page shows the simulated return and drawdown of a popular trend-following trading system. Notice that, compared to the previous thirty years, the range of run-up and drawdown has increased tremendously.

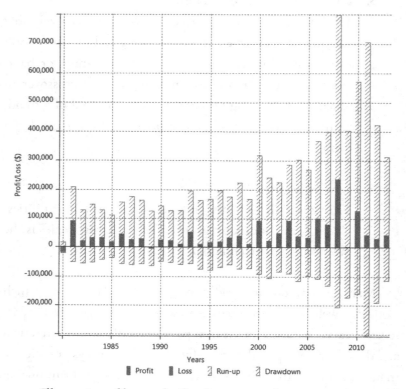

Illustration of how volatility has increased in recent years

Recent years have been marked by aggravated volatility. In his quarterly letter in 2012, Jeremy Grantham, founder and strategist for Boston-based GMO, which has a $120 billion portfolio, wrote that markets are volatile because of the "herding" behavior among traders who "go with the flow" of momentum. "Missing a big move, however unjustified it may be by fundamentals, is to take a very high risk of being fired. Career risk and the resulting herding it creates are likely to always dominate investing."

The growing popularity of high-frequency trading and leveraged-exchange traded products help fuel intraday and even longer-term volatility. Inability to grasp changing market conditions is damaging to the bottom line.

Tip: VIX is an excellent indicator for volatility. Watch not only the current value but also the overall trend of VIX.

Holding Period

A trading system can be designed for any holding period. The holding period can be as short as a few minutes or as long as several months or years.

Holding	**Length**
Intraday	Less than one day
Short Term	Days to weeks
Medium Term	Weeks to months
Long Term	Months to years

With recent technological advancement, day trading is more popular than ever. Some day traders hold the position for no more than an hour while looking at five-minute bars. Others enter the trade at the open and exit at the close of the day. Live data is a must for intraday trading.

Day traders enjoy tremendous leverage from their brokers. While the regular margin for a single E-Mini S&P contract is $5,000, a day trader could post a mere $500 for the same contract. It is crucial to point out that higher leverage comes with higher risk. It is a well-known phenomenon that the majority of day traders break their account in the first few months.

Day traders liquidate positions every day and sleep in cash every night. This is particularly comforting for those who fret about a black-swan event.

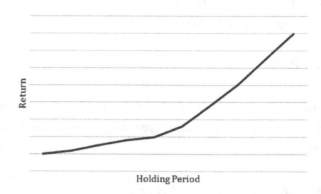

Illustration of how return increases with longer holding period

As a general principle, risk and return per trade are higher for longer holding periods. A day trader can generate one to two points per trade in E-Mini S&P, which is equivalent to $50 to $100 profit per trade before commissions and slippage. In contrast, it is not unusual for a short-term trade in E-Mini S&P (several days to a few weeks) to generate $500 to $1,000 profit per trade.

While risk and return are generally smaller, naturally there are more trade opportunities in intraday trading than in longer periods. As such, this results in higher commissions and slippages.

Tip: Successful traders tend to work within longer time frames than do day traders.

Instruments

No financial instrument is perfect to trade. It is crucial to understand the unique characteristics and behaviors of each instrument to build a trading system that matches a trader's personality.

1. **Stock**

   Stock is considered a relatively stable instrument. This is especially true with blue-chip stocks like those in the Dow 30. Smaller companies tend to be more susceptible to surprises.

2. **Exchange Trade Fund (ETF)**

   A typical ETF consists of several companies within the same industry. As such, it is less susceptible to surprises from a single company in the basket but behaves toward changes in the industry.

3. **Option**

   An option is an attractive instrument for traders looking for leverage. By putting up a fixed amount of capital, a trader can expect multiple returns.

4. **Foreign exchange**

   Foreign exchange (forex) is extremely volatile and reacts to a lot of external factors, such as major economic news, interest rates, changes in government policy such as devaluation, and so on.

5. **Futures**

A future is a financial contract requiring the buyer to buy and the seller to sell at a predetermined price on the agreed date. It can be classified into indices, financials, commodities (metal, meat, grains, softs), and forex. Each has its own personality and its place in a well-diversified portfolio. Appendix 3 shows a variety of popular futures.

Tip: Focus on certain instruments rather than being a jack of all trades and master of none.

Techniques

Abundant techniques are available to develop a trading system. Below are some common techniques.

Donchian Breakout

This is a simplified version of the system devised by Richard Donchian and was popularized by Richard Dennis and the Turtles. It is a simple, classic trend-following system and is also known as the Donchian Channels.

A buy signal is triggered with a price break-out of a twenty-day (or any) high, while a sell signal is based on a ten-day (or any) low. In contrast, a short signal is break-out of a twenty-day low, and a cover signal is break-out of a ten-day high.

The technique was particularly popular in the '80s, when the market trended with low volatility. With increased volatility, it is no longer as successful as before. See the previous graph showing risk and return of a Donchian system over more than thirty years.

Moving Average Crossover

Another popular trend-following technique is called moving average crossover. A buy signal is generated when a faster moving average (one that covers a shorter period, such as a ten-day moving average) crosses a slower moving average (such as a twenty-day moving average). The crossover signals that the trend is about to change; hence, a trade signal is generated. In our example, it is a sell signal when the ten-day moving average falls below the twenty-day moving average.

Volatility Open Range Breakout

This technique is a form of swing trading that focuses on immediate price action, without consideration of long-term changes. If the market moves significantly from the opening price, the odds favor it continuing to move in the same direction. This move may last for a while, but it presents adequate opportunity to profit. The trade is taken in the direction of the market on the principle that momentum precedes price action.

Chart Pattern Recognition

Chart pattern recognition is an early form of technical analysis that is based on behavioral theory. Driven by greed and fear, traders react with herd mentality. Patterns like double tops and bottom, head and shoulders, and triangle are reflections of these behaviors over the years. When a certain pattern is identified, trade is taken with the belief that history will repeat itself.

Size of System

In general, a trading system can be developed for varied sizes of accounts. A small account experiences a relatively higher drawdown than a larger account. Money management typically is more effective in a larger account because risk per trade decreases.

Account	**Size**
Small	$30,000
Medium	$60,000
Large	$100,000
Global	$200,000

A new trader is not advised to start with even a small account. Rather, start with a simulated account, better known as paper trade.

Order Entry

Different types of automation of order entry can execute signals generated by a trading system. While certain systems are best executed in a fully automated mode, some others may be better served in a fully manual order entry.

Manual—This is the most basic and well-known order entry. When the system generates a signal, the order is entered through the Internet. Alternatively, the order can be placed through a broker who executes the trade. This is a much more expensive proposition, but it appeals to certain traders, including those with the tendency to not follow the signals religiously, those who may easily get stressed out looking at daily account balances, or those whose trading systems require 24/7 monitoring.

Semi-automated—This is slightly more automated than the manual order entry. In a semi-automated system, when the signal is generated, the trader can place the order through the software itself rather than through the website of the broker.

Fully automated—This trading system is placed in the cloud and runs 24/7. When a signal is generated, an order is automatically placed without any human intervention. While certain trading systems, such as high-frequency trading, require this level of automation, most systems work fine with manual order entry. On any given day, data feeds could be interrupted, or the Internet connection could be down. Hence, fully automated systems must have an excellent risk-management mechanism built in. Fully automated order entry should not be equated with unattended trading.

The aim is to make money, not to be right.

~ Ned Davis

CHAPTER 8

Optimization

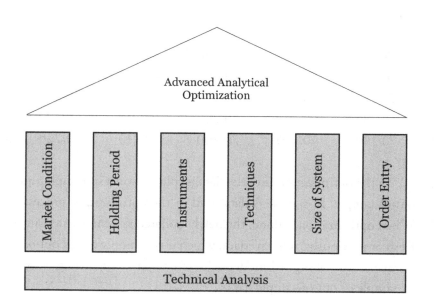

CHAPTER 8

Optimization

What is Optimization?

The legendary Turtle Traders used a simple Donchian system with a twenty-day break-out to achieve significant success. There were no questions about whether ten-day or thirty-day break-outs might yield better results. Similarly, a simple 50/200-day moving average crossover continues to be one of the gold standards in the nonoptimized trading system.

Optimization is a process of simulating the value of critical variables of a trading system to determine their most beneficial values. In the above example of a 50/200-day moving average crossover, the combinations shown below could be tested to see whether any might yield a more desirable result. With technological advancement, simulations can be conducted in a relatively short period of time.

30/80	30/190	30/200	30/210	30/220
40/180	40/190	40/200	40/210	40/220
50/180	50/190	50/200	50/210	50/220
60/180	60/190	60/200	60/210	60/220
70/180	70/190	70/200	70/210	70/220

In the optimization process, data is split between in-sample and out-of-sample. In-sample is data used in the optimization process. When optimization is done, the newly updated system is run using fresh or previously "unseen" data, which is commonly called out-of-sample. A well-designed model delivers similar results using either in-sample or out-of-sample data.

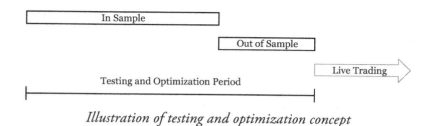

Illustration of testing and optimization concept

A well-known risk of optimization is curve fitting. In simple terms, curve fitting means excessive optimization in creating a "custom-designed" system with the greatest profit potential behind specific data and the time period. Back-testing results are no less than impressive, but the system is unreliable.

In general, curve fitting has two main causes.

1. Using too many rules instead of keeping it simple. The more rules in the system, the more "custom-fitted" the system is.
2. Using all available data for testing and leaving none for out-of-sample testing. Using the 50/200 moving average crossover, all available data (e.g., thirty years) is utilized to find the average combination that can yield impressive results.

Tip: If it is too good to be true, it is not true.

Nonoptimization

Advocates of nonoptimized trading systems believe that this is the purest trading system. Without any optimization, the system is deemed to be less influenced by the fallout of curve-fitting. Trading rules are generally based on conventional market wisdom or observation, such as golden cross with a 50/200 moving average crossover or "sell in May and go away." The *Stock Trader's Almanac* by Hirsch is a treasure for reference. A well-designed nonoptimized system can be extremely effective.

Illustration of nonoptimization

Walk Forward Analysis (WFA)

A WFA is an optimization technique that continues updating parameter values to incorporate the latest market conditions and testing it in the simulated "live." With a wealth of data available for optimization, the system has been "tested in real-life conditions" several times. It's no surprise that WFA is considered the gold standard among optimization techniques.

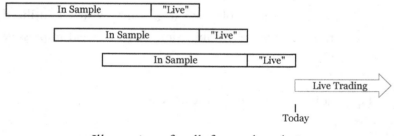

Illustration of walk forward analysis

Assume that historical data is available from 1990. The optimization can be subjected to ten years of in-sample data (1990-1999). Then, the system is updated using optimized parameters and is subjected to one year of out-of-sample data (2000). This process is repeated until it reaches out-of-sample data from 2013. At this point, the trading system has been subjected to fourteen instances of "simulated live" trading (from 2000 to 2013). If evaluation of the results is satisfactory and consistent, the system is run for the last time using in-sample data from 2004 to 2013 (ten years) and is ready for live trading in 2014.

Build, Rebuild, Compare (BRAC)

BRAC was coined by Keith Fitschen to optimize and test the reliability of a trading system. Using the earlier example with data from 1990, the system is subjected to in-sample data from 1990 to 2012 and is run with out-of-sample data from 2013. If both sets of results are similar, the system is considered reliable.

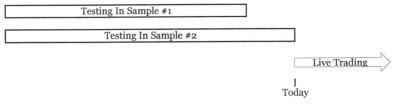

Illustration of build, rebuild, compare (BRAC)

Artificial Intelligence (AI)

Large institutions have been using artificial intelligence as their core systems for a long time. In a simplified version, similar technology is now available for the individual investor. Typical AI software combines the traditional method of building trading systems with AI techniques. When data is fed to the AI system, the advanced neural nets work to find the optimal algorithm for the expected outcome. The model is back-tested without much user intervention.

AI models should always be based on solid fundamental market understanding, such as interaction across Bonds, Gold, and the S&P Index. While there are some misconceptions that AI is the ultimate curve-fitting mechanism, nothing is further from the truth. It is not AI itself that curve fits but the developer of the model.

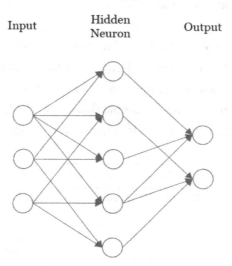

Illustration of neural network

Emotional control is the most essential factor in playing the market. Never lose control of your emotions when the market moves against you. Don't get too confident over your wins or too despondent over your losses.

~ Jesse Livermore

CHAPTER 9

Tools of the Trade

The right tools of the trade are critical components for a successful endeavor in mechanical trading. Investment in the tools should be considered as the cost of doing business.

Operating System — Most software is designed for Windows. Although some may work with virtualization in Mac OS, it is preferable to operate in a pure Windows environment.

Design and Testing — Design and testing software is the heart and soul in building a trading system where ideas are converted into rules, put to the test, and optimized. While most require coding skills, some are designed to work with plain English.

- TradeStation is an integrated trading platform and works with proprietary Easy Language. It is considered the gold standard in design and testing software. The platform is free for qualified clients of TradeStation Brokerage.

- MultiCharts is a standalone program based on Power Language. Its Power Language is compatible with Easy Language.
- AmiBroker can be the most cost-effective solution and yet the fastest analytical software in the market.

Data — Free end-of-day (EOD) data is available from several sources, including stock exchanges and Yahoo. Major brokerages like TradeStation, Interactive Brokers, and E*Trade offer their customers both EOD and intraday (ITD) live data feeds for a minimal fee, or even free for qualified customers.

Professionals subscribe to independent data suppliers for a reliable, high-quality, clean data feed. For those working at a tick level, E-Signal provides a more granular picture than those offered by brokerages. CSI Data and Premium Data are well-known names for EOD.

Advanced Analytical Software

NeuroShell Trader is an artificial intelligence software using state-of-the-art algorithms. The neural-network technology seeks to mimic the way human brains solve problems. In the same way humans apply lessons learned from past experiences to new problems, a neural network takes previous solutions to build a system of neurons to develop models, make predictions, and make decisions.

Market System Analyzer (MSA) uses Monte Carlo and position sizing to optimize performance of a trading system. Available trade data is run into thousands of permutations to generate a normal distribution of risk and return and to assess risk of ruin.

@Risk is a pure Monte Carlo add-on to Excel. It is suitable for systems done in Excel.

Idea Generation

- Books: Check out Amazon or Traders' Library.
  www.amazon.com
  www.traderslibrary.com

- Magazines: Subscribe to *Futures, Active Trader,* and *Stocks & Commodities.*
  www.futuresmag.com
  www.activetradermag.com
  www.traders.com

- Seminars: Join a free preview to see whether it is worth the investment, and check out online forums for reviews.
- Associations: Join local associations of technical analysts, such as Technical Analysts Society (Singapore), International Federation of Technical Analysts (IFTA).
- Google: Search for common terms on trading systems.

Brokerages

- Interactive Brokers (IB): Low-cost brokerage to trade markets around the world. Trading signals can be generated independently and sent to IB for execution.
  www.interactivebrokers.com

- Trade Station (TS): Integrated brokerage and trading platform that can be designed for full automation.
  www.tradestation.com

There is only one side of the market,
and it is not the bull side or the bear side,
but the right side.
~ Jesse Livermore

CHAPTER 10

Evaluating a Trading System

This chapter illustrates how to evaluate a trading system that is developed using MultiCharts.

Trading System	Bread and Butter
Market	Nontrending, low volatility
Holding Period	A few days
Instruments	Stock index
Techniques	Mean reversion
Size of System	$100k
Order Entry	Manual
Optimization	No optimization
Testing Period	2004 to 2013

Key Assumptions

- No capital withdrawal throughout testing period.
- Trade size is assumed to be fixed regardless of account size. This means as account size grows, risk reduces significantly.
- Results include commission and slippage (shown combined as commission in this example) of $50 per round trip.

Portfolio Performance Summary

	All Trades	Long Trades	Short Trades
Net Profit	524,921	358,243	166,677
Gross Profit	1,340,135	869,000	471,135
Gross Loss	(815,214)	(510,757)	(304,458)
Account Size Required	135,968	95,778	94,258
Return on Account	386.1	374.0	176.8
Return on Initial Capital	524.9	358.2	166.7
Profit Factor	1.64	1.70	1.55
Slippage Paid	-	-	-
Commission Paid	32,100	21,650	10,450
Open Net Profit	-	-	-
Max Portfolio Drawdown	(61,300)		
Max Portfolio Drawdown (%)	(21.0)		
Max Portfolio Close To Close Drawdown	(53,315)		
Max Portfolio Close To Close Drawdown (%)	(19.4)		
Return on Max Portfolio Drawdown	8.56		

- Net profit is $524,000 from 2004 to 2013 with profitable long and short trades.
- Profit factor (gross profit divided by gross loss) is 1.64, which is a good result.
- Maximum portfolio drawdown and maximum portfolio close-to-close drawdown are 21 percent and 19.4 percent, respectively. Both are acceptable for some but may be too high for others.

Typically, a good and reliable trading system should show balanced performance between long and short trades. Bread and Butter shows that net profit and profit factor are relatively balanced for long and short trades.

Portfolio Performance Ratios and Time Analysis

Portfolio Net Profit as % of Max Portfolio Drawdown	856.3
Trading Period	9 Yrs, 2 Mths, 22 Dys
Time in the Market	3 Yrs, 8 Mths, 15 Dys
Percent in the Market	40.1
Longest flat period	1 Mth, 23 Dys
Max Run-up Date	18/12/2013
Max Portfolio Drawdown Date	18/5/2012
Max Close To Close Drawdown Date	18/5/2012

Portfolio net profit as a percentage of maximum portfolio drawdown is at 856.3 percent. This is good, as we want to optimize profit generated versus drawdown.

This portfolio is only in the market for 40.1 percent of the time from 2004 to 2013. The less time the system is in the market, the less risk it is taking.

The longest flat period is one month and twenty-three days. This is the period when patience is tested to keep following the system while there is no trade.

Equity Curve Detailed

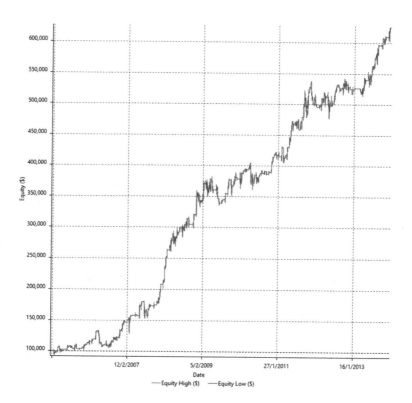

The overall equity curve looks decent with no severe or prolonged drawdown. It is important to notice several dips in the equity curve, which represent drawdowns. This is where the will to continue trading the system is tested. If available, smoothness of the growth in the equity curve can be measured by the K-ratio.

Equity Curve Detailed with Drawdown

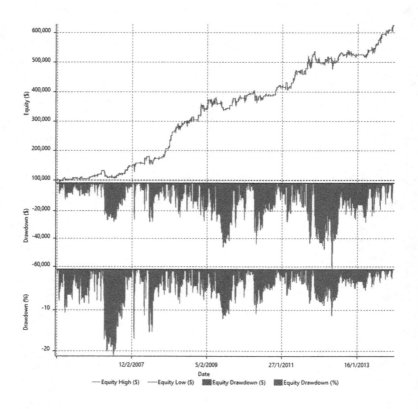

Notice a sharp point in the drawdown curve amounted to more than $60,000, representing more than 10 percent of equity. The largest drawdown, greater than 20 percent, happened relatively early. It is important to ask whether this amount of drawdown is acceptable to one's risk and reward value.

Total Trade Analysis

	All Trades	Long Trades	Short Trades
Total # of Trades	642	433	209
Total # of Open Trades	-	-	-
Number Winning Trades	328	234	94
Number Losing Trades	314	199	115
Percent Profitable	51.1	54.0	45.0
Avg Trade (win & loss)	818	827	797
Average Winning Trade	4,086	3,714	5,012
Average Losing Trade	(2,596)	(2,567)	(2,647)
Ratio Avg Win / Avg Loss	1.57	1.45	1.89

There are 642 trades, with 328 wins and 314 losses. Percent profitable is 51.1 percent. This is another important parameter to match with individual personality. Some prefer high percent-profitable ratios, while others can accept a low ratio.

The average trade results in profit of $818. This is crucial to cover commission and slippage. A relatively small average trade risk a nonprofitable system.

The average winning trade is $4,086, and the average losing trade is -$2,596. This is another good indication. Some can take lower winning trade versus losing trade, which would be compensated by a higher percent-profitable ratio.

Portfolio Monthly Period Analysis

Period	Net Profit	% Gain	Profit Factor	# Trades	Percent Profitable
Dec-13	15,435	2.5	3.55	7	85.7
Nov-13	4,311	0.7	2.95	3	66.7
Oct-13	9,290	1.6	1.99	7	57.1
Sep-13	9,650	1.6	387.00	3	66.7
Aug-13	21,147	3.7	2.65	14	64.3
Jul-13	18,515	3.4	8.03	7	71.4
Jun-13	3,095	0.6	1.15	11	45.5
May-13	8,670	1.6	4.56	4	50.0
Apr-13	14,970	2.9	2.10	10	50.0
Mar-13	(6,855)	(1.3)	-	4	-
Feb-13	-	-	-	-	-
Jan-13	1,950	0.4	1.00	1	100.0
Dec-12	(3,405)	(0.6)	(0.70)	5	40.0
Nov-12	(4,475)	(0.8)	(0.47)	5	20.0
Oct-12	7,814	1.5	1.64	12	58.3
Sep-12	790	0.2	1.11	7	28.6
Aug-12	(7,630)	(1.4)	(0.23)	5	60.0
Jul-12	29,665	5.9	11.41	8	87.5
Jun-12	(410)	(0.1)	(0.95)	3	66.7
May-12	(10,523)	(2.1)	(0.70)	18	27.8
Apr-12	(405)	(0.1)	(0.98)	9	33.3
Mar-12	15,597	3.1	2.33	10	60.0
Feb-12	2,065	0.4	83.60	2	50.0
Jan-12	(14,360)	(2.8)	(0.26)	7	14.3

Run through profit or loss every month. Gauge whether these monthly results meet risk and reward expectations. It is relatively simple to accept a string of profitable months (e.g., April 2013 to December 2013). However, it may be difficult to accept a $14,000 loss in a month (January 2012).

Portfolio Annual Period Analysis

Period	Net Profit	% Gain	Profit Factor	# Trades	Percent Profitable
2013	100,177	19.1	2.39	64	62.5
2012	14,723	2.9	1.10	83	45.8
2011	92,049	22.0	1.62	93	47.3
2010	39,371	10.4	1.47	63	50.8
2009	26,378	7.5	1.20	94	39.4
2008	144,549	69.6	3.04	71	56.3
2007	63,465	44.0	1.88	58	53.4
2006	35,202	32.3	1.67	63	57.1
2005	8,055	8.0	1.20	58	51.7
2004	950	1.0	1.00	1	100.0

The key assumption is no capital withdrawal. Trade size is kept fixed assuming capital utilization of $100,000. This means that profit of $100,000 in 2013 represents 100 percent profit for the year, while profit of $14,000 in 2012 represents 14 percent profit for the year.

It is good to see a profitable trading system on a year-on-year basis. In contrast, it may be more challenging to trade a system with a couple of consecutive loss years despite its overall profitability.

Average Profit by Month

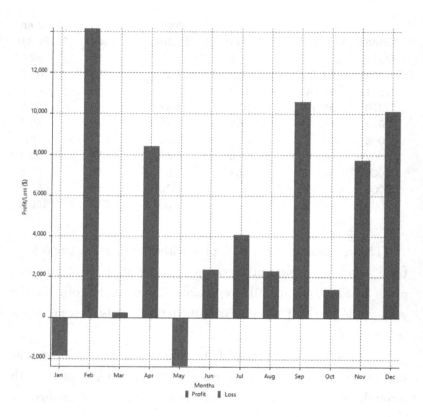

On average, the months of January and May are not profitable over the test period. The temptation not to trade for both months should be avoided without any fundamental reasons. This is an example of potential curve fitting.

Portfolio Analysis by Symbols

Market	Start Date	End Date	Net Profit	# Trades
EMD	5/1/2005	31/12/2013	79,520	146
GC2	9/12/2004	31/12/2013	132,260	140
ES	4/1/2005	31/12/2013	77,700	114
TF	4/1/2005	31/12/2013	88,841	124
DAX4	25/7/2006	30/12/2013	146,600	118

As shown in the above chart, all symbols are profitable. It is a good start, but it is not necessary to have all symbols to be profitable.

Market	Max. Equity Draw Down ($)	Max. Equity Draw Down(%)	Max. Equity Run-up($)	Max. Equity Run-up (%)	Avg. Monthly Return	Std. Dev. Of Monthly Return
EMD	(21,910)	(12.6)	84,130	84.9	736	3,526
GC2	(38,000)	(14.9)	167,630	189.8	1,236	4,715
ES	(14,175)	(8.7)	79,375	80.5	719	2,405
TF	(21,489)	(13.9)	93,631	97.9	823	3,191
DAX4	(58,950)	(25.8)	156,750	169.6	1,629	7,698

DAX4 is the most profitable, but it is also the most volatile. It has the highest drawdown in both dollar amount and percentage and the highest standard deviation of monthly return.

Market	Upside Potential	Sharpe Ratio	Avg. Win / Avg. Loss	Profit Factor	Percent Profitable
EMD	61.64	0.16	1.58	1.54	49.32
GC2	55.94	0.22	1.38	1.79	56.43
ES	134.42	0.21	1.85	1.98	51.75
TF	59.62	0.18	2.57	1.74	40.32
DAX4	31.15	0.21	1.09	1.49	57.63

DAX4 has the lowest upside potential and the lowest average win/loss. It is wise to see whether, without DAX4, the result matches better to the trader's personality.

Correlation Analysis by Symbols

Based on Daily Equity

	EMD	GC2	ES	TF	DAX4
EMD	1.00	0.10	0.38	0.35	0.28
GC2	0.10	1.00	0.02	0.02	0.04
ES	0.38	0.02	1.00	0.51	0.22
TF	0.35	0.02	0.51	1.00	0.21
DAX4	0.28	0.04	0.22	0.21	1.00

Based on Monthly Equity

	EMD	GC2	ES	TF	DAX4
EMD	1.00	0.32	0.27	0.31	0.11
GC2	0.32	1.00	0.03	0.10	(0.13)
ES	0.27	0.03	1.00	0.58	0.15
TF	0.31	0.10	0.58	1.00	0.18
DAX4	0.11	(0.13)	0.15	0.18	1.00

Based on Annual Equity

	EMD	GC2	ES	TF	DAX4
EMD	1.00	0.26	0.29	0.52	0.28
GC2	0.26	1.00	0.11	0.05	(0.18)
ES	0.29	0.11	1.00	0.15	0.58
TF	0.52	0.05	0.15	1.00	0.75
DAX4	0.28	(0.18)	0.58	0.75	1.00

On an annual basis, with the exception of DAX4 to TF, other symbols are minimally correlated to one another. Correlated symbols amplify both risk and revenue. It is always beneficial to have negatively correlated symbols to diversify, hence improving the risk-return ratio.

There are old traders, and there are bold traders,
but there are no old, bold traders.
~ Benjamin Hutchinson

CHAPTER 11

Managing Risk

Drawdown

Drawdown is a peak-to-trough decline in equity. It is seen as the most immediate and significant risk of a trading system. As such, drawdown is damaging not only to the bottom line but also to the psychological state of the trader. A prolonged or deep drawdown creates doubt about whether the system is working or whether the next signal should be taken.

System design on drawdown should factor in the risk tolerance of the trader, which can be measured either in absolute dollars or in percentages. Some can accept a drawdown of $10,000, and some can tolerate a drawdown of 10 percent. It is also crucial to factor in the length of the drawdown. The longer the drawdown lasts, the more it weighs on the trader's psychology.

The largest drawdown is always in the future, beyond what has been anticipated by the system design. Be prepared to take approximately double the anticipated drawdown.

Monthly Return and Drawdown ($)

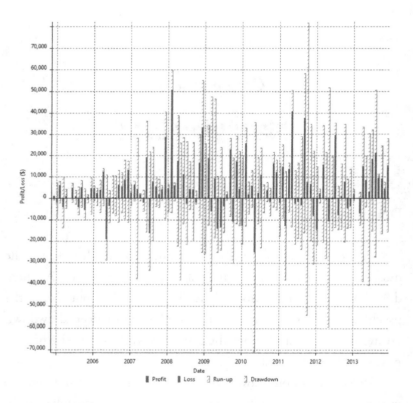

The chart illustrates monthly return and drawdown in terms of dollars. The highest drawdown is slightly more than $70,000 in 2010, before the month closes at -$25,000. There are a couple of other occasions with monthly drawdowns larger than $50,000.

Monthly Return and Drawdown (%)

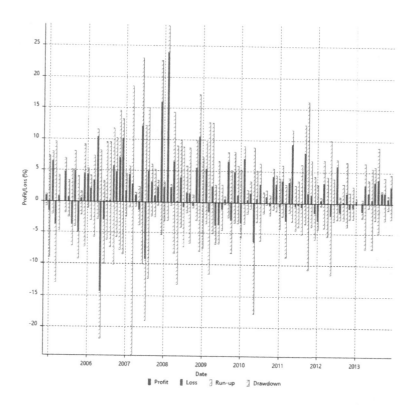

The chart illustrates monthly return and drawdown in terms of percentages, which should be observed in conjunction with the first drawdown in terms of dollars. The same drawdown of $70,000 in 2010 is around 17 percent of capital. While a 17 percent drawdown may be bearable, it might not be the same with a $70,000 drawdown.

Monte Carlo Simulation

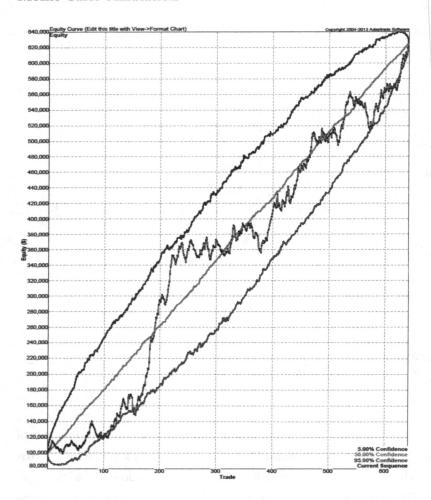

This Monte Carlo simulation is generated using Market System Analyzer (MSA). It is a tool to randomize the sequence of in-sample trades generated by the trading system. Based on hundreds or even thousands of simulations, MSA generates a range of estimated returns with a 95 percent confidence level.

Market System: Bread and Butter

Trading Parameters

Initial Account Equity: $100,000.00
Trading Vehicle: Futures
Initial Margin: $0.00
Round-turn slippage per contract: $0.00
Round-turn commissions and fees per contract: $0.00

Position Sizing Method: None
No. Contracts: From input data
Number of Monte Carlo Samples: 500

Key Results at Select Confidence Levels

Confidence (%)	Rate of Return (%)	Max Drawdown (%)	Return-DD Ratio	Mod. Sharpe Ratio
50	524.9	17.27	30.40	0.1758
60	524.9	19.19	27.36	0.1701
70	524.9	21.97	23.90	0.1639
80	524.9	24.98	21.01	0.1580
85	524.9	27.18	19.31	0.1552
90	524.9	30.27	17.34	0.1492
91	524.9	30.87	17.00	0.1473
92	524.9	31.39	16.72	0.1456
93	524.9	32.44	16.18	0.1434
94	524.9	33.51	15.67	0.1421
95	524.9	34.28	15.31	0.1407
96	524.9	36.99	14.19	0.1398
97	524.9	38.14	13.76	0.1383
98	524.9	40.89	12.84	0.1358
99	524.9	44.70	11.74	0.1252
100	524.9	53.15	9.876	0.1205

Monte Carlo Results at 95.00% Confidence

Total Net Profit: $524,920.80
Final Account Equity: $624,920.80
Return on Starting Equity: 524.9%
Profit Factor: 1.644

Max Number of Contracts: 1
Minimum Number of Contracts: 1
Average Number of Contracts: 1

Largest Winning Trade: $16,450.00
Largest Winning Trade (%): 7.755%
Average Winning Trade: $4,085.78
Average Winning Trade (%): 1.282%

Largest Losing Trade: ($16,550.00)
Largest Losing Trade (%): -15.19%
Average Losing Trade: ($2,596.22)
Average Losing Trade (%): -1.188%

Average Trade: $817.63
Average Trade (%): 0.2960%
Trade Standard Deviation: $4,152.75
Trade Standard Deviation (%): 2.202%

Win/Loss Ratio: 1.574
Win/Loss Ratio (%/%): 1.466
Max Consecutive Wins: 7
Max Consecutive Losses: 12

Worst Case Drawdown: ($61,047.00)
Worst Case Drawdown (%): 34.28%
Average Drawdown: ($7,718.42)
Average Drawdown (%): 2.901%

Return/Drawdown Ratio: 15.31
Modified Sharpe Ratio: 0.1407

From a general observation of the chart, Bread and Butter is fluctuating between the boundaries of 5 percent and 95 percent confidence. This indicates that the system is relatively volatile despite its strong result.

It is crucial to note that the confidence level is based on in-sample data. Hence, it assumes that the base trading system is solid to render a relevant simulation.

This Monte Carlo simulation result shows an expected drawdown of 34.28 percent at a 95 percent confidence level. This is a much different risk expectation versus the original result, without Monte Carlo, at 21 percent.

Risk of ruin is the possibility for a trading system to start with deep drawdown that consumes all of its initial capital. Even a solid trading system may hit a rough patch. By randomizing the sequence of trades, the Monte Carlo simulation shows the potential risk of ruin of a trading system.

Significance Test Settings

Number of rules and/or restrictions in trading system or method: 0
Confidence level for confidence intervals around average trade: 95.00%

Significance Test Results

Number of Trades: 642
Number of Degrees of Freedom: 642
Average trade at 95.00% confidence: $817.63 +/- 269.61
Worst-case average trade at 95.00% confidence: $548.02
Probability that average trade is greater than zero: > 99.95%

>Trades pass statistical significance test at specified confidence level<

In the significance test shown above, the possibility that average trade is greater than zero is 99.95 percent. This should provide extra confidence to trade the system.

More Watch Outs

Future Leak

This is an unintentional logic error that occurs when coding the trading system by looking at future data to generate signals. For example, the entry price for a signal depends on the high and low of the same day. As the entry price is decided after the fact, the result of the back-test is outstanding but is not tradable in the real world. A system like AmiBroker has a specific function to help detect future leak.

Slippage and Commission

There are costs involved that have to be factored into the evaluation. Slippage is higher in an illiquid market because of the unfavorable bid-ask spread. Incorporating slippage and commission into a system with minimal profitability can create a losing system.

Tradability

In the futures market, closing price is determined by a predetermined formula and is published minutes after the official closing time. A system with an entry signal based on closing price may not be tradable in a runaway market without pullback if the order is entered long after the closing time.

Bulls make money, bears make money,
pigs get slaughtered.
~ Anonymous

Chapter 12

Portfolio of Trading Systems

A portfolio of trading systems is a combination of trading systems designed to optimize risk-return ratio. It is crucial to note that the systems should be minimally correlated or preferably uncorrelated. By adding uncorrelated systems, the portfolio diversifies its risk.

A properly designed portfolio increases return at a higher rate than it increases risk. When one trading system in the portfolio fails, the other trading systems are expected to compensate for the failure.

Trading System:	Bread and Butter	Morning Star	Silver Light
Market:	Non Trending Low Volatility	Trending High Volatility	Trending Low Volatility
Holding Period:	Few Days	Few Weeks	Few Months
Instruments:	Stock Index	Commodities	Commodities
Techniques:	Mean Reversion	Momentum	Trend Following
Size of System:	$100k	$80k	$100k
Order Entry:	Manual	Manual	Manual
Optimization:	None	None	None

This chapter illustrates how to evaluate a portfolio of trading systems. The first trading system, Bread and Butter, has been introduced in an earlier chapter. Key assumptions are the same as shown in Chapter 10. This portfolio trades 47 symbols.

Portfolio Performance Summary

	Bread and Butter	Morning Star	Silver Light	All Trades
Net Profit	524,921	212,430	620,022	1,404,275
Gross Profit	1,340,135	752,150	1,677,260	3,871,686
Gross Loss	(815,214)	(539,721)	(1,057,238)	(2,467,411)
Account Size Required	135,968	233,547	273,599	652,628
Return on Account	386.1	91.0	226.6	215.2
Return on Initial Capital	524.9	265.5	620.0	501.5
Profit Factor	1.64	1.39	1.59	1.57
Slippage Paid	0	0	0	0
Commission Paid	32,100	36,950	55,775	129,125
Open Net Profit	0	16,665	16,020	32,684
Max Drawdown	(61,300)	(60,035)	(99,586)	(126,214)
Max Drawdown (%)	(21.0)	(47.7)	(24.2)	(22.6)
Max Close To Close Drawdown	(53,315)	(61,159)	(51,403)	(80,976)
Max Close To Close Drawdown (%)	(19.4)	(43.4)	(17.5)	(12.6)
Return on Max Drawdown	9	4	6	11

- Net profit is $1,404,000 from 2004 to 2013 with profitable long and short trades.
- Profit factor (gross profit divided by gross loss) is 1.57, which is a good result.
- Maximum portfolio drawdown and maximum portfolio close-to-close drawdown are 22.6 percent and 12.6 percent, respectively. Notice how combined maximum portfolio close-to-close drawdown is much better than in an individual system. When systems are minimally correlated, drawdown reduces significantly.

Portfolio Performance Summary

Net Profit	Bread and Butter	Morning Star	Silver Light	All Trades
2013	100,177	(27,927)	14,538	86,788
2012	14,723	23,462	24,142	62,327
2011	92,049	11,869	37,605	141,523
2010	39,371	93,693	121,144	253,878
2009	26,378	12,698	(3,995)	35,081
2008	144,549	86,004	230,829	461,383
2007	63,465	35,527	74,698	173,691
2006	35,202	5,022	95,817	136,041
2005	8,055	(18,482)	29,211	18,784
2004	950	7,228	12,052	20,230
Average	52,492	22,909	63,604	138,973

Net Profit %	Bread and Butter	Morning Star	Silver Light	All Trades
2013	100.2	(34.9)	14.5	31.0
2012	14.7	29.3	24.1	22.3
2011	92.0	14.8	37.6	50.5
2010	39.4	117.1	121.1	90.7
2009	26.4	15.9	(4.0)	12.5
2008	144.5	107.5	230.8	164.8
2007	63.5	44.4	74.7	62.0
2006	35.2	6.3	95.8	48.6
2005	8.1	(23.1)	29.2	6.7
2004	1.0	9.0	12.1	7.2
Average	52.5	28.6	63.6	49.6

The overall portfolio averages 49.6 percent annual return on base capital of $280,000. In years when one system is not performing well, the other two systems more than offset the impact.

Equity Curve Detailed with Drawdown

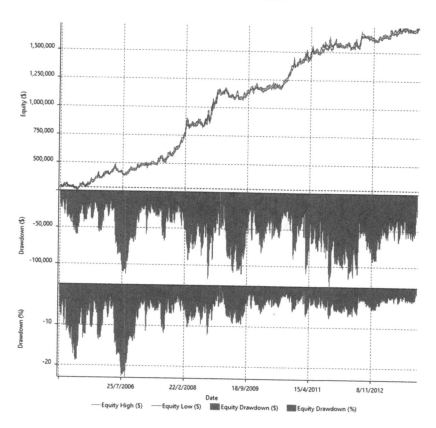

There are more than adequate occasions when the drawdown exceeds $100,000 per month. This requires strength of will to continue. Notice how drawdown stays at relatively the same level while overall equity increases behind capital gain.

Equity Run Up and Drawdown

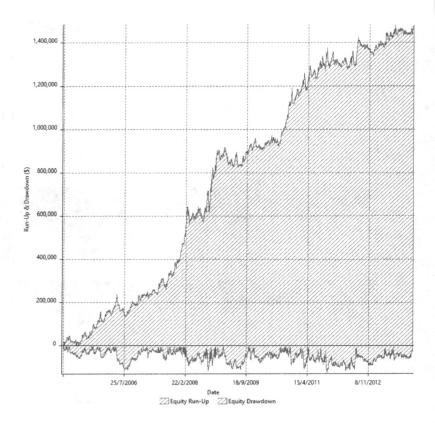

With the same scale for both equity and drawdown, it is clear that the drawdown is more palatable in the later years. There are no significant increases beyond the $100,000 mark.

Portfolio Monthly Period Analysis

Period	Net Profit	% Gain	Profit Factor	# Trades	Percent Profitable
Dec-13	24,461	1.4	1.88	52	48.1
Nov-13	2,256	0.1	1.09	43	39.5
Oct-13	(6,118)	(0.4)	(0.81)	46	54.3
Sep-13	(3,494)	(0.2)	(0.84)	42	35.7
Aug-13	4,351	0.3	1.11	53	43.4
Jul-13	(2,448)	(0.1)	(0.94)	48	37.5
Jun-13	17,878	1.1	1.33	56	39.3
May-13	7,989	0.5	1.25	46	39.1
Apr-13	36,942	2.3	2.08	46	52.2
Mar-13	(6,615)	(0.4)	(0.72)	42	42.9
Feb-13	3,907	0.2	1.14	39	33.3
Jan-13	7,679	0.5	1.27	40	40.0
Dec-12	22,839	1.4	1.81	40	40.0
Nov-12	(11,050)	(0.7)	(0.65)	41	36.6
Oct-12	(11,896)	(0.7)	(0.76)	53	45.3
Sep-12	(9,576)	(0.6)	(0.66)	37	37.8
Aug-12	(14,690)	(0.9)	(0.64)	37	27.0
Jul-12	116,294	7.6	7.76	48	66.7
Jun-12	(58,312)	(3.7)	(0.22)	50	22.0
May-12	55,792	3.6	2.10	54	55.6
Apr-12	(22,059)	(1.4)	(0.59)	51	39.2
Mar-12	3,615	0.2	1.08	52	26.9
Feb-12	562	0.0	1.02	33	33.3
Jan-12	(9,192)	(0.6)	(0.79)	41	41.5

Naturally, the portfolio monthly return fluctuates at a higher level than in an individual system. While it is comforting to see a profitable month, a loss of $58,000 in June 2012 weighs heavily.

Monte Carlo Simulation

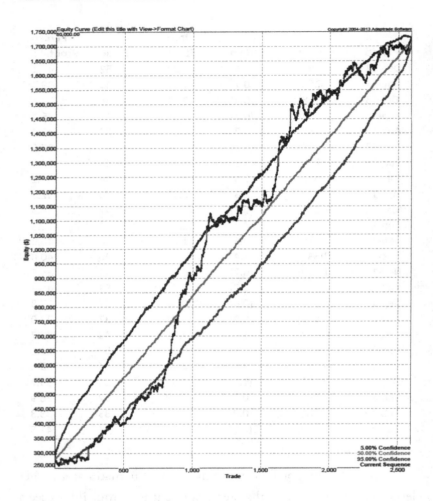

After many iterations, equity fluctuates around the confidence level lines with no evident deep drawdown.

Market System: Portfolio

Trading Parameters

Initial Account Equity: $280,000.00
Trading Vehicle: Futures
Initial Margin: $0.00
Round-turn slippage per contract: $0.00
Round-turn commissions and fees per contract: $0.00

Position Sizing Method: None
No. Contracts: From input data
Number of Monte Carlo Samples: 500

Key Results at Select Confidence Levels

Confidence (%)	Rate of Return (%)	Max Drawdown (%)	Return-DD Ratio	Mod. Sharpe Ratio
50	513.2	9.166	55.99	0.1203
60	513.2	10.07	50.94	0.1182
70	513.2	10.85	47.30	0.1158
80	513.2	12.18	42.13	0.1128
85	513.2	12.81	40.06	0.1108
90	513.2	14.16	36.25	0.1091
91	513.2	14.43	35.57	0.1083
92	513.2	14.78	34.73	0.1077
93	513.2	15.29	33.56	0.1072
94	513.2	15.52	33.07	0.1066
95	513.2	15.88	32.31	0.1062
96	513.2	16.79	30.57	0.1047
97	513.2	17.82	28.80	0.1043
98	513.2	19.67	26.09	0.1021
99	513.2	20.49	25.04	0.1008
100	513.2	29.21	17.57	0.0943

Monte Carlo Results at 95.00% Confidence

Total Net Profit: $1,436,959.28
Final Account Equity: $1,716,959.28
Return on Starting Equity: 513.2%
Profit Factor: 1.581

Max Number of Contracts: 2
Minimum Number of Contracts: 1
Average Number of Contracts: 1

Largest Winning Trade: $65,425.00
Largest Winning Trade (%): 5.888%
Average Winning Trade: $3,578.81
Average Winning Trade (%): 0.4199%

Largest Losing Trade: ($16,550.00)
Largest Losing Trade (%): -5.144%
Average Losing Trade: ($1,647.59)
Average Losing Trade (%): -0.2433%

Average Trade: $553.74
Average Trade (%): 0.0713%
Trade Standard Deviation: $4,056.43
Trade Standard Deviation (%): 0.6789%

Win/Loss Ratio: 2.172
Win/Loss Ratio (%/%): 2.076
Max Consecutive Wins: 7
Max Consecutive Losses: 18

Worst Case Drawdown: ($77,209.55)
Worst Case Drawdown (%): 15.88%
Average Drawdown: ($7,045.30)
Average Drawdown (%): 0.9234%

Return/Drawdown Ratio: 32.31
Modified Sharpe Ratio: 0.1062

Compared to an individual system like Bread and Butter, the portfolio shows much improved drawdown at every level of confidence. This shows how diversification reduces risk.

Final Thoughts

Geoffrey Chaucer once noted, "Right as diverse pathes leden the folk the righte wey to Rome." Building a robust portfolio of trading systems is one way to deliver consistent return. Some may take a few years, and some may take longer. It is the journey that matters.

Live your passion to embark on this path of least resistance to consistent profitability. Smell the roses along the up market and the down market. Doors are always open for those who knock. Wake up each day knowing that today is one day closer to the finish line.

Godspeed . . .

If I have seen farther than others,
it is by standing upon the shoulders of giants.
~ Isaac Newton

APPENDIX 1

References

ARONSON, D. (2006). *Evidence-Based Technical Analysis: Applying the Scientific Method and Statistical Inference to Trading Signals.* 1st edition. New York: Wiley.

ARONSON, D. and MASTERS, T. (2013). *Statistically Sound Machine Learning for Algorithmic Trading of Financial Instruments: Developing Predictive-Model-Bases Trading Systems Using TSSB.* 1st edition. Create Space.

BANDY, H. (2009). *Advanced AmiBroker.* Tucson: Blue Owl Press.

BANDY, H. (2008). *Introduction to AmiBroker.* Tucson: Blue Owl Press.

BANDY, H. (2013). *Mean Reversion Trading Systems.* Tucson: Blue Owl Press.

BANDY, H. (2011). *Modelling Trading System Performance.* Tucson: Blue Owl Press.

BANDY, H. (2007). *Quantitative Trading Systems.* Tucson: Blue Owl Press.

CONNORS, L. and ALVAREZ, C. (2008). *Short-Term Trading Strategies that Work.* New York: Wiley.

CONNORS, L., ALVAREZ, C., and CONNORS RESEARCH (2009). *High Probability ETF Trading: 7 Professional Strategies to Improve Your ETF Trading.* New York: Wiley.

CONNORS, L., ALVAREZ, C., and CONNORS RESEARCH (2000). *How Markets Really Work: Quantitative Guide to Stock Market Behavior.* 2nd edition. New York: Wiley.

ELDER, A. (2002). *Come Into My Trading Room: A Complete Guide to Trading.* 1st edition. New York: Wiley.

ELDER, A. (2006). *Entries & Exits: Visits to 16 Trading Rooms.* 1st edition. New York: Wiley.

ELDER, A. (2008). *Sell and Sell Short.* 1st edition. New York: Wiley.

ELDER, A. (1993). *Trading for a Living: Psychology, Trading Tactics, Money Management.* 1st edition. New York: Wiley.

FITSCHEN, K. (2013). *Building Reliable Trading Systems: Tradable Strategies That Perform As They Backtest and Meet Your Risk-Reward Goals.* 1st edition. New York: Wiley.

HILL, J.R., PRUITT, G., and HILL, L. (2000). *The Ultimate Trading Guide.* New York: Wiley.

KIRKPATRICK, C.D. and DAHLQUIST, J. (2010). *Technical Analysis: The Complete Resource for Financial Market Technicians.* 2nd edition. Upper Saddle River: Pearson Education.

LEFEVRE, E. and LOWENSTEIN, R. (2006). *Reminiscences of a Stock Operator.* New York: Wiley.

RASCHKE, L.B. and CONNORS, L.A. (1996). *Street Smarts: High Probability Short-Term Trading Strategies.* 1st edition. Malibu: M. Gordon Publishing Group.

SCHWAGER, J.D. (1995). *Schwager on Futures: Technical Analysis.* 1st edition. New York: Wiley.

SCHWAGER, J.D. (2003). *Stock Market Wizards: Interviews with America's Top Stock Traders.* 1ˢᵗ edition. New York: Wiley.

SCHWAGER, J.D. (1994). *The New Market Wizards: Conversations with America's Top Traders.* 1ˢᵗ edition. New York: Wiley.

STEENBARGER, B.N. (2002). *The Psychology of Trading: Tools and Techniques for Minding Markets.* 1ˢᵗ edition. New York: Wiley.

THARP, V. (2000). *Financial Freedom through Electronic Day Trading.* 1ˢᵗ edition. New York: Wiley.

THARP, V. (1998). *Trade Your Way to Financial Freedom.* 1ˢᵗ edition. New York: Wiley.

Definitions from MultiCharts

Account Size Required: This field calculates the amount of money you must have in your account to trade the strategy. This value is calculated using the following formula: Account Size Required = Absolute Value of Maximum Drawdown (Trade Close to Trade Close).

Gross Loss: The total sum of every losing trade generated by a strategy. This characteristic of a strategy is most important yet often overlooked. It should be noted that net profit increases not only when gross profit improves but also when gross loss is reduced. Analyzing and working over losing trades is an extremely important part of trading-strategy analysis.

Gross Profit: The total sum of every profitable trade generated by a strategy.

Longest Flat Period: The longest period the strategy refrains from trading; the system patience measure. Keep in mind that a long flat period means the trader must have enough patience to follow the strategy (an important value to consider).

Max Portfolio Close-to-Close Drawdown: Displays the greatest loss drawdown from the previous highest equity run-up, closed trade to closed trade, looking across all trades during the specified period. If a new closed trade equity high occurs, we reset the low equity value to zero, looking for the next maximum drawdown from that point.

Max Close-to-Close Drawdown Date: The date and time of the maximum close-to-close drawdown.

Max Portfolio Drawdown: Displays the greatest loss drawdown from the previous highest equity run-up, bar to bar, looking around all trades during the specified period. If a new bar equity run-up high occurs, the low equity value is reset to zero so that the next maximum drawdown can be calculated from that point.

Max Portfolio Drawdown Date: The date and time of the maximum portfolio drawdown.

Max Run-Up Date: The date and time of the maximum run-up.

Net Profit: The overall dollar profit or loss achieved by the trading strategy in the test period.

Percent in the Market: The trading period divided by the time in the market.

Profit Factor: The dollar amount a trading strategy made for every dollar it lost. This value is calculated by dividing gross profits by gross losses.

Return on Account: The sum of money you would make compared to the sum of money required to trade the strategy, after considering the margin and margin calls. This value is calculated by dividing the net profit by the account size required.

Return on Initial Capital: Displays the percentage return of the total net profit to the initial starting capital (including commissions and slippage if specified) during the specified period. Return on Initial Capital = Total Net Profit divided by Initial Capital.

Return on Max Portfolio Drawdown: The portfolio net profit divided by its maximum portfolio drawdown.

Time in the Market: The time that the strategy is in market. The greater the amount of time the strategy is in the market, the more the strategy equity will be exposed to market moves, and thus the greater the risk.

Trading Period: The length of the test period.

APPENDIX 3

Futures from Premium Data

Category	Futures	Symbol	$ Per Point	$ Margin
Metal	Gold	GC	100	2,035
Metal	Copper	HG	250	1,823
Metal	Palladium	PA	100	1,650
Metal	Platinum	PL	50	2,363
Metal	Silver	SI	50	1,100
Energy	Crude Oil	CL	1,000	1,265
Energy	Heating Oil	HO	42,000	3,190
Energy	Natural Gas	NG	10,000	1,925
Energy	Reformulated Gas	RB	42,000	1,045
Indices	E-Mini Midcap 400	EMD	100	2,475
Indices	E-Mini S&P	ES	50	880
Indices	Nikkei	NK	5	7,700
Indices	E-Mini Nasdaq 100	NQ	20	4,758
Indices	E-Mini Russell 2000	TF	100	2,025

Indices	E-Mini Dow Jones	YM	5	990
Currency	Australian Dollar	AD	100,000	7,150
Currency	British Pound	BP	62,500	3,300
Currency	Canadian Dollar	CD	100,000	3,465
Currency	Dollar Index	DX	1,000	3,465
Currency	Euro Currency	EC	125,000	8,030
Currency	Euro Dollar	ED	2,500	1,750
Currency	Japanese yen	JY	125,000	2,400
Currency	Mexican Peso	MP	50,000	1,148
Currency	Swiss Franc	SF	125,000	1,620
Soft	Cocoa	CC	10	1,980
Soft	Cotton	CT	500	3,425
Soft	Coffee	KC	375	3,135
Soft	Lumber	LB	110	3,850
Soft	Orange Juice	OJ	150	1,688
Soft	Sugar	SB	1,120	1,375
Financial	5-Year Note	FV	1,000	4,125
Financial	2-Year Note	TU	2,000	2,750
Financial	10-Year Note	TY	1,000	3,850
Financial	30-Year Bond	US	1,000	1,485
Grains	Bean Oil	BO	600	3,375
Grains	Corn	C	50	935
Grains	KC Wheat	KW	50	2,530
Grains	Oats	O	50	9,900
Grains	Rough Rice	RR	20	2,700
Grains	Soybeans	S	50	5,610
Grains	Bean Meal	SM	100	341
Grains	Wheat	W	50	1,430
Meat	Feeder Cattle	FC	500	2,310
Meat	Live Cattle	LC	400	1,890
Meat	Lean Hogs	LH	400	3,575

APPENDIX 4

Links

@Risk: www.palisade.com
AmiBroker: www.amibroker.com
Blue Owl Press: www.blueowlpress.com
Commodity Systems, Inc.: www.csidata.com
E*Trade: www.etrade.com
eSignal: www.esignal.com
Interactive Brokers: www.interactivebrokers.com
Market System Analyzer: www.adaptrade.com
MultiCharts: www.multicharts.com
NeuroShell Trader: www.neuroshell.com
Norgate Investor Services: www.premiumdata.net
StockCharts.com: www.stockcharts.com
TradeStation: www.tradestation.com